Ancestors of Barbara Ann Bell

Generation 1

1.   **Barbara Ann Bell**, daughter of William Robert Bell and Alma Louise Akerman was born on 07 Jun 1958 in San Diego, California. She married **Billy Darrell Maynard**, son of Billy Edward Maynard and Karen Ann Hensley on 14 Oct 1976 in Wylie, Texas. He was born on 05 Nov 1956 in McKinney, Texas.

More About Billy Darrell Maynard:
Occupation: Machinist

Generation 2

2.   **William Robert Bell**, son of Joseph Bell and Emily Louise Connally was born on 13 Jul 1922 in Coalgate, Oklahoma. He died on 04 Nov 1981 in Texas. He married **Alma Louise Akerman**, daughter of Donald Akerman and Theresa Diester on 11 Aug 1951 in McAllister, Oklahoma.

3.   **Alma Louise Akerman**, daughter of Donald Akerman and Theresa Diester was born on 11 Nov 1930 in Sacred Heart, Oklahoma. She died on 22 Dec 2010 in Dallas, Texas.

More About William Robert Bell:
Burial: Saint Paul Catholic Cemetery, Saint Paul, Collin County, Texas Living In: 1981 in Wylie, Texas
Military Service: April 29, 1943 - January 19, 1946, U.S. Navy Seabee

Notes for William Robert Bell:
Served with the 90th USNCB and the 95th USNCB during World War Two. William participated in the battle for Iwo Jima with the 90th USNCB.

More About Alma Louise Akerman:
Burial: 27 Dec 2010 in Saint Paul Catholic Cemetery, Saint Paul, Collin County, Texas

Alma Louise Akerman and William Robert Bell had the following child:
  1.   i. Barbara Ann Bell, daughter of William Robert Bell and Alma Louise Akerman was born on 07 Jun 1958 in San Diego, California. She married Billy Darrell Maynard, son of Billy Edward Maynard and Karen Ann Hensley on 14 Oct 1976 in Wylie, Texas. He was born on 05 Nov 1956 in McKinney, Texas.

Generation 3

4.   **Joseph Bell**, son of William Bell and Ann Kirkwood Patterson was born on 13 Jun 1883 in Krebs, Indian Territory (Present Day Oklahoma). He died on 27 Oct 1958 in Coalgate, Oklahoma. He married **Emily Louise Connally**, daughter of Charles Clay Connaly and Willie Etta Jenkins on 18 Nov 1906 in Choctaw Nation, Indian Territory (Present Day Oklahoma).

5.   **Emily Louise Connally**, daughter of Charles Clay Connaly and Willie Etta Jenkins was born on 10 Aug 1885 in Huntsville, Alabama. She died on 07 Oct 1951 in Coalgate, Oklahoma.

More About Joseph Bell:
Burial: 30 Oct 1958 in Coalgate, Oklahoma
Occupation: 1900 in Coalgate, Choctaw Nation, Indian Territory (Present Day Oklahoma); Coal Miner
Occupation: 1910 in Coalgate, Coal County, Oklahoma; Pharmacist in Drug Store

Occupation: 1920 in Coalgate, Coal County, Oklahoma; Drug Store Proprietor
Occupation: 1930 in Coalgate, Coal County, Oklahoma; Druggist in Retail Drug Store
Occupation: 1940 in Coalgate, Coal County, Oklahoma; Druggist in Drug Store

Notes for Joseph Bell:
Owned his own drugstore in Coalgate, Oklahoma.
Funeral Record gives birth date as June 13, 1882. Headstone gives year of birth as 1882.
World War One and World War Two draft registrations give date of birth as June 13, 1883.
Marriage record indicates birth year of 1883.

More About Emily Louise Connally:
Burial: 09 Oct 1951 in Coalgate Cemetery, Coalgate, Oklahoma, Rev. Frank Warnke
officiating Occupation: 1940 in Coalgate, Coal County, Oklahoma; Assistant in Drug Store

Emily Louise Connally and Joseph Bell had the following children:

    i.   Louise H. Bell, daughter of Joseph Bell and Emily Louise Connally was born on 01 Dec 1907 in Oklahoma. She died on 18 Dec 1988 in Kaufman County, Texas. She married Lee Shugar. He was born about 1905. She married Leo K. Hughes on 26 Jan 1929 in Durant, Bryan County, Oklahoma. He was born about 1905.

        More About Louise H. Bell:
        Burial: Saint Paul Cemetery, Saint Paul, Texas

        More About Leo K. Hughes and Louise H. Bell:
        Marriage Fact: Married by William N. Shall, Minister of First Prebyterian Church, Durant

    ii.   Joseph Connally Bell, son of Joseph Bell and Emily Louise Connally was born on 26 Oct 1910 in Coalgate, Oklahoma. He died on 21 Sep 1979 in Las Vegas, Nevada.

        More About Joseph Connally Bell:
        Burial: Woodlawn Cemetery, Las Vegas, Nevada
        Military Service: Enlisted in U.S. Army at Los Angeles, California on November 20, 1943

2.   iii. William Robert Bell, son of Joseph Bell and Emily Louise Connally was born on 13 Jul 1922 in Coalgate, Oklahoma. He died on 04 Nov 1981 in Texas. He married Alma Louise Akerman, daughter of Donald Akerman and Theresa Diester on 11 Aug 1951 in McAllister, Oklahoma. She was born on 11 Nov 1930 in Sacred Heart, Oklahoma. She died on 22 Dec 2010 in Dallas, Texas.

6.   **Donald Akerman**, son of John Nickolas Akerman and Cora Etta Waldrop was born on 24 Aug 1900 in Arkansas. He died on 24 Jul 1937 in Oklahoma. He married **Theresa Diester**.

7.   **Theresa Diester**, daughter of John Thomas Diester and Cynthia Elizabeth Carr was born on 30 Apr 1895 in Texas. She died on 14 Nov 1986 in Oklahoma.

More About Donald Akerman:
Burial: Sacred Heart Cemetery, Asher, Oklahoma

More About Theresa Diester:
Burial: Sacred Heart Cemetery, Asher, Oklahoma

Theresa Diester and Donald Akerman had the following children:

    i.   Billy Akerman.

    ii.   Chris Akerman.

    iii.   Mary Akerman.

    iv.   Francis Akerman, son of Donald Akerman and Theresa Diester was born on 05 Jul 1925. He died on 28 Jan 1956.

        More About Francis Akerman:
        Burial: Sacred Heart Cemetery, Asher, Oklahoma
        Military Service: ; Corporal, United States Marine Corps, World War Two

    v.   Michael D. Akerman, son of Donald Akerman and Theresa Diester was born on 04 Jan 1927. He died on 07 Apr 2010 in Seminole, Oklahoma.

    vi.

        More About Michael D. Akerman:
        Burial: 09 Apr 2010 in Sacred Heart Cemetery, Kanawa, Oklahoma

3.   vi. Alma Louise Akerman, daughter of Donald Akerman and Theresa Diester was born on 11 Nov 1930 in Sacred Heart, Oklahoma. She died on 22 Dec 2010 in Dallas, Texas. She married William Robert Bell, son of Joseph Bell and Emily Louise Connally on 11 Aug 1951 in McAllister, Oklahoma. He was born on 13 Jul 1922 in Coalgate, Oklahoma. He died on 04 Nov 1981 in Texas.

Generation 4

8.   **William Bell**, son of Joseph Bell and Elizabeth McLachlan was born on 16 May 1845 in Glasgow, Lanarkshire, Scotland. He died on 18 Mar 1924 in Coalgate, Oklahoma. He married **Ann Kirkwood Patterson**, daughter of Robert Patterson and Barbara Speirs on 01 Jan 1866 in Carnbuslang, Lanarkshire, Scotland.

9.   **Ann Kirkwood Patterson**, daughter of Robert Patterson and Barbara Speirs was born on 15 May 1846 in Silverbanks,Cambuslang, Lanarkshire, Scotland. She died on 07 Jan 1934 in Coalgate, Oklahoma.

10.

More About William Bell:
Burial: 20 Mar 1924 in Coalgate Cemetery, Coalgate, Oklahoma
Immigration: Mar 1869 in From Scotland to Maryland
Occupation: 1866 in Cambuslang, Lanarkshire, Scotland; Coal Miner
Occupation: 07 Jul 1870 in Election District number 16, Allegany County, Maryland; Miner Occupation: 1879 in Krebs, Indian Territory (Present Day Oklahoma); Coal Miner
Occupation: 1900 in Coalgate, Choctaw Nation, Indian Territory (Present Day Oklahoma); Coal Miner
Occupation: 1910 in Coalgate, Oklahoma; Retired
Occupation: 1920 in Coalgate, Oklahoma; Retired

More About Ann Kirkwood Patterson:
Burial: 09 Jan 1934 in Coalgate Cemetery, Coalgate, Oklahoma
Immigration: 22 Jul 1871 in Arrived in New York, New York on ship "India"

Living In: 02 Apr 1871 Ann and her children are living with her parents in Silverbanks, Cambuslang, Lanarkshire, Scotland.
Living In: Jun 1880 Delta, Keokuk County, Iowa
Living In: 1930 Coalgate, Coal County, Oklahoma

Notes for Ann Kirkwood Patterson:
Headstone has May 16, 1846 for date of birth.

Ann Kirkwood Patterson and William Bell had the following children:

i.   Barbara Patterson Bell, daughter of William Bell and Ann Kirkwood Patterson was born on 03 Mar 1867 in Silverbanks, Cambuslang, Lanarkshire, Scotland. She died on 12 Mar 1936 in Oklahoma City, Oklahoma. She married Alexander Bowie. He was born about 22 Dec 1858 in Pennsylvania. He died on 04 Mar 1889 in McAlester, Indian Territory (Present Day Oklahoma). She married Robert H. Brown on 13 Sep 1893 in Thurber, Erath County, Texas. He was born on 08 May 1867 in Scotland. He died on 25 Dec 1950 in St Louis, Missouri.

More About Barbara Patterson Bell:
Burial: 15 Mar 1936 in Coalgate Cemetery, Coalgate, Oklahoma
Emigration: 22 Jul 1871 in Arrived in New York, New York on ship "India"

Notes for Barbara Patterson Bell:
Headstone has February 24, 1868 for date of birth.

More About Alexander Bowie:
Burial: North McAlester Cemetery, McAlester, Oklahoma

More About Robert H. Brown:
Burial: 29 Dec 1950 in Coalgate Cemetery, Coalgate, Oklahoma
Living In: 1935 Oklahoma City, Oklahoma
Occupation: 1900 in Coalgate, Choctaw Nation, Indian Territory (Present Day Oklahoma); Coal Miner
Occupation: 1910 in Coalgate, Coal County, Oklahoma; Coal Mine Fire Boss Occupation: 1920 in Coalgate, Coal County, Oklahoma; Miner
Occupation: 1930 in Coalgate, Coal County, Oklahoma; District Inspector of Coal Mines
Occupation: Bet. 1931-1947; Chief Mine Inspector for Oklahoma

Notes for Robert H. Brown:
Arrived in United States from Scotland in 1881.

----

ii.   Joseph Bell, son of William Bell and Ann Kirkwood Patterson was born on 22 Mar 1869 in Dalserf, Lanarkshire, Scotland. He died on 08 May 1882 in Indian Territory (Present Day Oklahoma).

More About Joseph Bell:
Burial: McAlester Cemetery, McAlester, Oklahoma

iii.   William Bell, son of William Bell and Ann Kirkwood Patterson was born in 1872 in Maryland. He died in 1954 in Illinois. He married Margaret Kerr, daughter of Thomas Kerr about 1893. She was born on 08 Jul 1873 in Scotland. She died on 17 Mar 1921 in Collinsville, Illinois. He married Rose Kaufman about 1923. She was born on 30 Aug 1890 in Carlinville, Illinois. She died in Jan 1980 in Alton, Madison County, Illinois.

More About William Bell:
Burial: Bethalto United Methodist Church Cemetery, Bethalto, Illinois
Occupation: 1900 in Precinct 10, Las Animas County, Colorado; Coal Miner
Occupation: 1910 in Collinsville, Madison County, Illinois; Coal Miner
Occupation: 1920 in Collinsville, Madison County, Illinois; Coal Miner
Occupation: 1930 in Bethalto, Madison County, Illinois; Coal Miner

Notes for William Bell:
In 1900 William was working in Las Animas County, Colorado while Margaret was living in Cerrillos, New Mexico with their children.

More About Margaret Kerr:
Burial: 20 Mar 1921 in St. John Cemetery, Collinsville, Illinois
Living In: 1900 Cerrilos, Santa Fe County, New Mexico

Notes for Margaret Kerr:
Margaret was living, with her children, in Cerrillos, New Mexico in 1900 while William was working in Las Animas County, Colorado.

More About Rose Kaufman:
Burial: Bethalto United Methodist Church Cemetery, Bethalto, Illinois

iv.   Robert H. Bell, son of William Bell and Ann Kirkwood Patterson was born on 08 Sep 1874 in Maryland. He died on 07 Nov 1902. He married Mary M. Boozle on 16 May 1897 in Muscogee County, Indian Territory, (present day Oklahoma).

More About Robert H. Bell:
Burial: Coalgate Cemetery, Coalgate, Oklahoma
Occupation: 1900 in Madrid, Santa Fe County, New Mexico; Coal Miner

Notes for Robert H. Bell:
1900 U.S. census shows Robert was married about 1897 and still married in 1900. He was living as a boarder in 1900.

v.   Elizabeth Bell, daughter of William Bell and Ann Kirkwood Patterson was born in Aug 1879 in Iowa. She died on 11 Aug 1960 in Coalgate, Oklahoma. She married John McInnis, son of John McInnes and Mary Belle VanBrocklin in Feb 1902 in Coalgate, Choctaw Nation, Indian Territory (Present Day Oklahoma). He was born on 15 Dec 1878 in Ohio. He died on 20 Aug 1918 in Coalgate, Oklahoma.

More About Elizabeth Bell:

Burial: 14 Aug 1960 in Coalgate Cemetery, Coalgate, Oklahoma
Occupation: 1900 in Coalgate, Choctaw Nation, Indian Territory (Present
Day Oklahoma); Saleswoman in Drugstore
Occupation: 1920 in Coalgate, Coal County, Oklahoma; Saleswoman in
Drugstore Occupation: 1930 in Coalgate, Coal County, Oklahoma; Retail Dry
Goods Saleswoman

Notes for Elizabeth Bell:
Elizabeth McInnis Claimed by death at Home. Services for Elizabeth McInnis were
held at the First Methodist church at 2 o'clock Sunday afternoon by Daniel Forbes,
Mrs. McInnis and her husband, John McInnis, came to Coalgate 66 years ago from
Krebs, and he preceded her in death 42 years ago, She died quietly at sleep at her
home here Thursday. Mrs. McInnis worked for many years in the Corner Drug store
and Margaret Covington's ready to wear store here. She was active in the Coalgate
Garden Club. Linger Longer Embroidery Club, and the order of the Eastern Star.
Surviving are two sons, C. R, McInnis, R. M. McInnis, and a daughter, Mrs. Peggy
Helvey, one brother, Jim Bell of Henrietta, five grandchildren, and five great
grandchildren. Pall bearers were W. E. Larecy, W. H. Bailey, Eddie Cox, Arthur
Pope, Jim Farrimond, and Elmo Childers. Among the out of town relatives
attending the services were Mrs. Agnes Hinshaw and Jean Booth of Ft. Smith,
Ark; Mr. and Mrs. Billy Bell and daughter, and Bobbie Jean McInnis of Oklahoma
City; Louise Sugar of Londoner, MD, Mrs. George Bell of Oklahoma City; Emma
Doris Wyche of Durant, Jean Patterson and Annie Mowatt of Oklahoma City; Bob
Patterson, John Hall and daughter of Henrietta; Mr. and Mrs. John Jones, Mrs.
Ted Henderson of Wapanucha; Mrs. Harry Miller and granddaughter, Cynthia,
Mrs. Ethel Harwell of Ada; Sam Covington, Mr. & Mrs. Bill Cowan of Oklahoma
City. Burial was at Coalgate cemetery with Slater funeral home directing.

More About John McInnis:
Burial: Coalgate Cemetery, Coalgate, Oklahoma
Occupation: 1900 in Coalgate, Choctaw Nation, Indian Territory (Present
Day Oklahoma); Bookkeeper
Occupation: 1910 in Coalgate, Coal County, Oklahoma; Livery Stable Prioprietor

Notes for John McInnis:
Headstone has last name spelled McInnis.

vi.   James P. Bell, son of William Bell and Ann Kirkwood Patterson was born on 17
Dec 1880 in Iowa. He died in Aug 1966 in Oklahoma. He married Isabel Liddle on
05 Jun 1909 in Coalgate, Coal County, Oklahoma. She was born about 1886 in
Indian Territory (Present Day Oklahoma).

More About James P. Bell:
Living In: 1930 As a boarder in Detroit, Michigan.
Living In: 1966 Henryetta, Oklahoma
Occupation: 1900 in Coalgate, Choctaw Nation, Indian Territory (Present
Day Oklahoma); Coal Miner
Occupation: 1910 in Coalgate, Oklahoma; Coal Miner
Occupation: 1918 in Henryetta, Oklahoma; Working for Blackstone Coal Mine
in Henryetta, Oklahoma

Occupation: 1920 in Henryetta, Oklahoma; Coal Miner
Occupation: 1930 in Detroit, Michigan; Factory Worker
Occupation: 1940 in Henryetta, Oklahoma; Field Representative for Coal Company

Notes for James P. Bell:

World War One draft registration gives December 17, 1879 as date of birth.
Social Security death index gives December 17, 1880 as date of birth. James is
not on 1880 U.S. census taken June 22, 1880 in Iowa. World War Two draft
registration gives date of birth as December 17, 1880.

More About Isabel Liddle:
Living In: 1930 Henryetta. Oklahoma

Notes for Isabel Liddle:
First name is Isabel on marriage certificate.

4.   vii. Joseph Bell, son of William Bell and Ann Kirkwood Patterson was born on 13 Jun 1883
          in Krebs, Indian Territory (Present Day Oklahoma). He died on 27 Oct 1958 in
          Coalgate, Oklahoma. He married Emily Louise Connally, daughter of Charles Clay
          Connaly and Willie Etta Jenkins on 18 Nov 1906 in Choctaw Nation, Indian Territory
          (Present Day Oklahoma). She was born on 10 Aug 1885 in Huntsville, Alabama. She
          died on 07 Oct 1951 in Coalgate, Oklahoma.

     viii. George Patterson Bell, son of William Bell and Ann Kirkwood Patterson was born
          on 07 May 1886 in Krebs, Indian Territory (Oklahoma). He died on 04 Sep 1949 in
          Gorman, Texas. He married Blanche Lee Hanlin on 26 Feb 1907 in Coalgate,
          Choctaw Nation, Indian Territory (Present Day Oklahoma). She was born on 06
          Mar 1887 in Mississippi. She died on 27 Jan 1963 in Oklahoma.

          More About George Patterson Bell:
          Burial: 06 Sep 1949 in Coalgate Cemetery, Coalgate, Oklahoma
          Living In: 1940 George and Blanche are living with their son in law and daughter
          in Hugo, Oklahoma.
          Occupation: 1910 in Hobart, Kiowa County, Oklahoma; Sewing Machine Agent
          Occupation: 1916 in Okmulgee, Okmulgee County, Oklahoma; Coal Miner
          Occupation: 1920 in Okmulgee, Okmulgee County, Oklahoma; Clerk in Loan
          Office
          Occupation: 1930 in Oklahoma City, Oklahoma; Lease and Royalty Prosessor
          Occupation: 1940 in Hugo, Choctaw County, Oklahoma; Independant Oil Lease
          Processor
          Occupation: 1942 in Hugo, Choctaw County, Oklahoma; Self Employed
          Occupation: 1949 in Hugo, Choctaw County, Oklahoma; Oil Lease Broker

          More About Blanche Lee Hanlin:
          Burial: Coalgate Cemetery, Coalgate, Oklahoma

          Notes for Blanche Lee Hanlin:
          Social Security death index gives year of death as 1963. Headstone gives year
          of death as 1962.

10. **Charles Clay Connaly** was born in Alabama. He married **Willie Etta Jenkins**.

11. **Willie Etta Jenkins** was born on 16 Sep 1850 in Madison County, Alabama. She died on 23 Jun 1925 in Coalgate, Oklahoma.
More About Willie Etta Jenkins:
Burial: 26 Jun 1925 in Coalgate Cemetery, Coalgate, Oklahoma

Willie Etta Jenkins and Charles Clay Connaly had the following child:

    5.   i. Emily Louise Connally, daughter of Charles Clay Connaly and Willie Etta Jenkins was born on 10 Aug 1885 in Huntsville, Alabama. She died on 07 Oct 1951 in Coalgate, Oklahoma. She married Joseph Bell, son of William Bell and Ann Kirkwood Patterson on 18 Nov 1906 in Choctaw Nation, Indian Territory (Present Day Oklahoma). He was born on 13 Jun 1883 in Krebs, Indian Territory (Present Day Oklahoma). He died on 27 Oct 1958 in Coalgate, Oklahoma.

12. **John Nickolas Akerman**, son of John Nickolas Akerman and Julia Anna Lux was born on 11 Sep 1868 in Indiana. He died on 04 Jun 1951 in Lyford, Texas. He married **Cora Etta Waldrop**, daughter of James Waldrop and Ann McDonald on 09 Mar 1892 in Lafayette County, Arkansas.

13. **Cora Etta Waldrop**, daughter of James Waldrop and Ann McDonald was born on 22 Jul 1875 in Arkana, Louisiana. She died on 09 Oct 1936 in Willacy County, Texas.

More About John Nickolas Akerman:
Burial: 08 Jun 1951 in Raymondville Cemetery, Raymondville,
Texas Cause Of Death: Cerebral Hemorrhage
Occupation: 1880; Working on Farm, Union, Arkansas
Occupation: 1900; Farmer, Lafayette County. Arkansas

More About Cora Etta Waldrop:
Burial: 10 Oct 1936 in Raymondville Cemetery, Raymondville,
Texas Cause Of Death: Cerebral Hemorrhage

Cora Etta Waldrop and John Nickolas Akerman had the following children:

       i.   George D. Akerman, son of John Nickolas Akerman and Cora Etta Waldrop was born in Feb 1893 in Arkansas.

      ii.   James Akerman, son of John Nickolas Akerman and Cora Etta Waldrop was born in Nov 1894 in Arkansas.

     iii.   Julia A. Akerman, daughter of John Nickolas Akerman and Cora Etta Waldrop was born in Oct 1896 in Arkansas.

     iv.   Lawrence F. Akerman, son of John Nickolas Akerman and Cora Etta Waldrop was born in May 1898 in Arkansas.

      v.   John Akerman, son of John Nickolas Akerman and Cora Etta Waldrop was born about 1900 in Arkansas.

    6.   vi. Donald Akerman, son of John Nickolas Akerman and Cora Etta Waldrop was born on 24 Aug 1900 in Arkansas. He died on 24 Jul 1937 in Oklahoma. He married Theresa Diester. She was born on 30 Apr 1895 in Texas. She died on 14 Nov 1986 in Oklahoma.

     vii.   Andy Akerman, son of John Nickolas Akerman and Cora Etta Waldrop was born about 1904 in Arkansas.

    viii. Nicholas Akerman, son of John Nickolas Akerman and Cora Etta Waldrop was born about 1906 in Arkansas.

    ix. Pat Akerman, son of John Nickolas Akerman and Cora Etta Waldrop was born about 1911 in Oklahoma.

    x. Joseph Akerman, son of John Nickolas Akerman and Cora Etta Waldrop was born about 1914 in Oklahoma.

    xi. Charles Akerman, son of John Nickolas Akerman and Cora Etta Waldrop was born about 1916 in Oklahoma.

    xii. Catherine Akerman, daughter of John Nickolas Akerman and Cora Etta Waldrop was born about 1917 in Oklahoma.

14.   **John Thomas Diester**, son of John Christopher Diester and Catherine Caroline Bueltaman was born on 22 Apr 1850 in Missouri. He married **Cynthia Elizabeth Carr**.

15.   **Cynthia Elizabeth Carr** was born in 1851 in Alabama. She died on 23 Mar 1939.

More About John Thomas
Diester: Occupation: Farmer

Cynthia Elizabeth Carr and John Thomas Diester had the following children:

    i. Ema Diester, daughter of John Thomas Diester and Cynthia Elizabeth Carr was born about 1877 in Texas.

    ii. William Diester, son of John Thomas Diester and Cynthia Elizabeth Carr was born about 1879 in Texas.

    iii. Rosa L. Diester, daughter of John Thomas Diester and Cynthia Elizabeth Carr was born in Sep 1881 in Texas.

    iv. John T. Diester, son of John Thomas Diester and Cynthia Elizabeth Carr was born in Feb 1884 in Texas.

    v. Annie B. Diester, daughter of John Thomas Diester and Cynthia Elizabeth Carr was born in Mar 1886 in Texas.

    vi. Phillip H. Diester, son of John Thomas Diester and Cynthia Elizabeth Carr was born in Aug 1890 in Texas.

8.   vii. Theresa Diester, daughter of John Thomas Diester and Cynthia Elizabeth Carr was born on 30 Apr 1895 in Texas. She died on 14 Nov 1986 in Oklahoma. She married Donald Akerman. He was born on 24 Aug 1900 in Arkansas. He died on 24 Jul 1937 in Oklahoma.

Generation 5

16.   **Joseph Bell** was born about 1818 in England. He died before 01 Jan 1866 in Scotland. He married **Elizabeth McLachlan**, daughter of Hugh McLachlan on 10 May 1840 in Glasgow, Lanarkshire, Scotland.

17.   **Elizabeth McLachlan**, daughter of Hugh McLachlan was born about 1817 in Lanarkshire, Scotland. She died before 01 Jan 1866 in Scotland.

More About Joseph Bell:
Living In: 1841 With his father in law at Gibson St. 3, Glasgow St. James, Lanarkshire, Scotland.
Living In: 1851 20 Warrenstone Close, Edinburgh High Church Parish, Midlothian County, Scotland.
Occupation: 1841 in Glasgow St. James, Lanarkshire, Scotland; Blacksmith
Occupation: 1851 in Edinburgh High Church Parish, Midlothian County, Scotland; Blacksmith and Chain Maker

Elizabeth McLachlan and Joseph Bell had the following children:

      i.   George Bell, son of Joseph Bell and Elizabeth McLachlan was born about 1841 in Glasgow, Lanarkshire, Scotland.

9.   ii. William Bell, son of Joseph Bell and Elizabeth McLachlan was born on 16 May 1845 in Glasgow, Lanarkshire, Scotland. He died on 18 Mar 1924 in Coalgate, Oklahoma. He married Ann Kirkwood Patterson, daughter of Robert Patterson and Barbara Speirs on 01 Jan 1866 in Carnbuslang, Lanarkshire, Scotland. She was born on 15 May 1846 in Silverbanks,Cambuslang, Lanarkshire, Scotland. She died on 07 Jan 1934 in Coalgate, Oklahoma.

      iii.   Joseph Bell, son of Joseph Bell and Elizabeth McLachlan was born about 1849 in Glasgow, Lanarkshire, Scotland.

18.   **Robert Patterson**, son of Robert Patterson and Margaret McAlpine was born about Jun 1807 in Rutherglen, Lanarkshire, Scotland. He died on 15 Mar 1873 in Silverbanks, Cambuslang, Lanarkshire, Scotland. He married **Barbara Speirs**.

19.   **Barbara Speirs**, daughter of Robert Speirs and Agnes Naismith was born about 1814 in Tobcross, Lanarkshire, Scotland. She died on 04 Nov 1884 in Rutherglen, Lanarkshire, Scotland.

More About Robert Patterson:
Living In: 1861 Silverbanks, Cambuslang, Lanarkshire, Scotland
Living In: 02 Apr 1871 Silverbanks, Cambuslang, Lanarkshire, Scotland
Occupation: 1861 in Cambuslang, Lanarkshire, Scotland; Coal Miner
Occupation: 02 Apr 1871 in Cambuslang, Lanarkshire, Scotland; Coal Miner

Notes for Robert Patterson:
Death record says he was 65 and 9/12 years old at the time of his
death. Parents names are on his death record.

Notes for Barbara Speirs:
Death record says she was 70 years old at the time of her death.

Barbara Speirs and Robert Patterson had the following children:

      i.   Robert Patterson, son of Robert Patterson and Barbara Speirs was born on 17 Mar 1835 in Cambuslang, Lanark, Scotland.

      ii.   Agnes Naismith Patterson, daughter of Robert Patterson and Barbara Speirs was born on 28 Feb 1837 in Cambuslang, Lanarkshire, Scotland.

      iii.   Margaret McAlpine Patterson, daughter of Robert Patterson and Barbara Speirs was born on 02 Aug 1839 in Rutherglen, Lanarkshire, Scotland.

iv. Archibald Speirs Patterson, son of Robert Patterson and Barbara Speirs was born on 17 Sep 1841 in Rutherglen, Lanarkshire, Scotland.

v. Barbara Patterson, daughter of Robert Patterson and Barbara Speirs was born on 19 Jul 1843 in Rutherglen, Lanarkshire, Scotland.

9. vi. Ann Kirkwood Patterson, daughter of Robert Patterson and Barbara Speirs was born on 15 May 1846 in Silverbanks,Cambuslang, Lanarkshire, Scotland. She died on 07 Jan 1934 in Coalgate, Oklahoma. She married William Bell, son of Joseph Bell and Elizabeth McLachlan on 01 Jan 1866 in Carnbuslang, Lanarkshire, Scotland. He was born on 16 May 1845 in Glasgow, Lanarkshire, Scotland. He died on 18 Mar 1924 in Coalgate, Oklahoma.

vii. James Speirs Patterson, son of Robert Patterson and Barbara Speirs was born on 19 Jul 1848 in Cambuslang, Lanarkshire, Scotland.

viii. Gilbert Patterson, son of Robert Patterson and Barbara Speirs was born on 18 May 1851 in Rutherglen, Lanarkshire, Scotland. He died between 12 Jun 1900-25 Apr 1910. He married Ann Patterson, daughter of Charles Patterson and Janet Neil on 1 Jan 1873 in Silverbanks, Cambuslang, Lanark, Scotland. She was born in Aug 1847 in Scotland. She died after 25 Apr 1910.

More About Gilbert Patterson:
Emigration: 01 Feb 1882 in New York, New York
Occupation: 1873 in Cambuslang, Lanark, Scotland; Coal Miner
Occupation: 1900 in Township 5, Choctaw Nation, Indian Territory (present day Oklahoma); Coal Miner

Notes for Gilbert Patterson:
Arrived in New York, New York February 1, 1882 on SS Italy.

Transcription of birth record in Scotland gives first name as Gabriel.

More About Ann Patterson:
Emigration: 1888
Living In: 1910 Krebs Ward 3, Pittsburg County, Oklahoma
Occupation: 1873 in Cambuslang, Lanark, Scotland; Paper Mill Worker

ix. Elizabeth Patterson, daughter of Robert Patterson and Barbara Speirs was born on 15 Jun 1854 in Rutherglen, Lanarkshire, Scotland.

x. William Kirkwood Patterson, son of Robert Patterson and Barbara Speirs was born on 14 Apr 1858 in Rutherglen, Lanarkshire, Scotland. He died on 30 Aug 1937 in Detroit, Michigan. He married Elizabeth Duncan on 06 Feb 1882 in McAlester, Indian Territory (Present Day Oklahoma). She was born in Oct 1859 in Rutherglen, Lanarkshire, Scotland. She died on 20 Jul 1943 in Pleasant Valley (near Schulter), Oklahoma.

More About William Kirkwood Patterson:

Burial: 02 Sep 1937 in Westlawn Cemetery, Henryetta, Oklahoma
Occupation: 1900 in Coalgate, Choctaw Nation, Indian Territory (Present Day
Oklahoma); Coal Miner
Occupation: 1910 in Murray, Coal County, Oklahoma; Coal Miner
Occupation: 1920 in Murray, Coal County, Oklahoma; Coal Miner
Occupation: 1930 in Shulter, Okmulgee County, Oklahoma; Retired

Notes for William Kirkwood Patterson:
Was visiting his daughter, Agnes, in Detroit, Michigan when he died.
1910 and 1930 U.S. census gives year of Immigration as 1881.

Patterson family Bible gives date of birth as April 14, 1858. Scotland Births
and Baptisms gives date of birth as April 16, 1858.

More About Elizabeth Duncan:
Burial: 23 Jul 1943 in Westlawn Cemetery, Henryetta,
Oklahoma Emigration: 01 Feb 1882 in New York, New York

Notes for Elizabeth Duncan:
Arrived in New York, New York February 1, 1882 on SS Italy. Escorted on
voyage by Gilbert Patterson.

More About William Kirkwood Patterson and Elizabeth Duncan:
Marriage Fact: Married by Reverend Will Hicks

24. **John Nickolas Akerman** was born about 1847 in France. He married **Julia Anna Lux** on 26
Nov 1867 in Madison, Jefferson County, Indiana.

25. **Julia Anna Lux** was born about 1850 in France.

More About John Nickolas Akerman:
Living In: 1880 in Union, Arkansas
Occupation: 1880; Farmer, Union, Arkansas

Julia Anna Lux and John Nickolas Akerman had the following children:
12.   i. John Nickolas Akerman, son of John Nickolas Akerman and Julia Anna Lux was born on
            11 Sep 1868 in Indiana. He died on 04 Jun 1951 in Lyford, Texas. He married Cora
            Etta Waldrop, daughter of James Waldrop and Ann McDonald on 09 Mar 1892 in
            Lafayette County, Arkansas. She was born on 22 Jul 1875 in Arkana, Louisiana. She
            died on 09 Oct 1936 in Willacy County, Texas.
        ii. Mary Akerman, daughter of John Nickolas Akerman and Julia Anna Lux was
             born about 1870 in Indiana.

       iii. Elizabeth Akerman, daughter of John Nickolas Akerman and Julia Anna Lux
             was born about 1871 in Indiana.

        iv. Rosa Akerman, daughter of John Nickolas Akerman and Julia Anna Lux was
             born about 1876 in Indiana.

v. Leo Akerman, son of John Nickolas Akerman and Julia Anna Lux was born about 1878 in Indiana.

vi. George D. Akerman, son of John Nickolas Akerman and Julia Anna Lux was born on 12 Dec 1880 in Indiana. He married Lillian E. Kirsch, daughter of Balser Kirsch and Mary Rute on 20 Jan 1939 in Jackson County, Indiana. She was born on 22 Jun 1883. He married (unknown). She died in 1928.

More About George D. Akerman:
Occupation: 1939 in North Vernon, Indiana; mechanic

26.   **James Waldrop**. He married **Ann McDonald**.

27.   **Ann McDonald**.
Ann McDonald and James Waldrop had the following child:
13.   i. Cora Etta Waldrop, daughter of James Waldrop and Ann McDonald was born on 22 Jul 1875 in Arkana, Louisiana. She died on 09 Oct 1936 in Willacy County, Texas. She married John Nickolas Akerman, son of John Nickolas Akerman and Julia Anna Lux on 09 Mar 1892 in Lafayette County, Arkansas. He was born on 11 Sep 1868 in Indiana. He died on 04 Jun 1951 in Lyford, Texas.

28.   **John Christopher Diester** was born on 15 Aug 1808 in Germany. He died in Jun 1855. He married **Catherine Caroline Bueltaman**.

29.   **Catherine Caroline Bueltaman** was born about 1811 in Germany.

Catherine Caroline Bueltaman and John Christopher Diester had the following children:
i. Masthias Diester, son of John Christopher Diester and Catherine Caroline Bueltaman was born about 1835 in Germany.

ii. Joseph P. Diester, son of John Christopher Diester and Catherine Caroline Bueltaman was born about 1841 in Germany.

iii. Anna Diester, daughter of John Christopher Diester and Catherine Caroline Bueltaman was born about 1846 in Germany.

iv. Catherine Diester, daughter of John Christopher Diester and Catherine Caroline Bueltaman was born about 1849 in Germany.

14.   v. John Thomas Diester, son of John Christopher Diester and Catherine Caroline Bueltaman was born on 22 Apr 1850 in Missouri. He married Cynthia Elizabeth Carr. She was born in 1851 in Alabama. She died on 23 Mar 1939.

Generation 6

34.   **Hugh McLachlan** was born about 1776 in Scotland.

Hugh McLachlan had the following child:
17.   i. Elizabeth McLachlan, daughter of Hugh McLachlan was born about 1817 in Lanarkshire, Scotland. She died before 01 Jan 1866 in Scotland. She married Joseph Bell on 10 May 1840 in Glasgow, Lanarkshire, Scotland. He was born about 1818 in England. He died before 01 Jan 1866 in Scotland.

36.   **Robert Patterson**. He married **Margaret McAlpine**.

37.   **Margaret McAlpine**.

Margaret McAlpine and Robert Patterson had the following child:

    18.   i. Robert Patterson, son of Robert Patterson and Margaret McAlpine was born about Jun 1807 in Rutherglen, Lanarkshire, Scotland. He died on 15 Mar 1873 in Silverbanks, Cambuslang, Lanarkshire, Scotland. He married Barbara Speirs. She was born about 1814 in Tobcross, Lanarkshire, Scotland. She died on 04 Nov 1884 in Rutherglen, Lanarkshire, Scotland.

38.   **Robert Speirs**. He married **Agnes Naismith**.

39.   **Agnes Naismith**.

40.

More About Robert Speirs:

Occupation: Coal Miner

Agnes Naismith and Robert Speirs had the following child:

    19.   i. Barbara Speirs, daughter of Robert Speirs and Agnes Naismith was born about 1814 in Tobcross, Lanarkshire, Scotland. She died on 04 Nov 1884 in Rutherglen, Lanarkshire, Scotland. She married Robert Patterson. He was born about Jun 1807 in Rutherglen, Lanarkshire, Scotland. He died on 15 Mar 1873 in Silverbanks, Cambuslang, Lanarkshire, Scotland.

Ancestors of Billy Darrell Maynard

Generation 1

2.   **Billy Darrell Maynard**, son of Billy Edward Maynard and Karen Ann Hensley was born on 05 Nov 1956 in McKinney, Texas. He married **Barbara Ann Bell**, daughter of William Robert Bell and Alma Louise Akerman on 14 Oct 1976 in Wylie, Texas. She was born on 07 Jun 1958 in San Diego, California.

More About Billy Darrell Maynard:
Occupation: Machinist

Generation 2

4.   **Billy Edward Maynard**, son of Gilbert Edward Maynard and Ina Mae Campbell was born on 14 Jul 1932 in Texas. He married **Karen Ann Hensley**, daughter of Grover Cecil Hensley and Letha Arwaner White on 24 Dec 1955 in Wylie, Texas.

5.   **Karen Ann Hensley**, daughter of Grover Cecil Hensley and Letha Arwaner White was born on 17 Jun 1937 in Durant, Oklahoma.

More About Billy Edward Maynard:
Occupation: Machinist

Karen Ann Hensley and Billy Edward Maynard had the following child:

1.   i. Billy Darrell Maynard, son of Billy Edward Maynard and Karen Ann Hensley was born on 05 Nov 1956 in McKinney, Texas. He married Barbara Ann Bell, daughter of William Robert Bell and Alma Louise Akerman on 14 Oct 1976 in Wylie, Texas. She was born on 07 Jun 1958 in San Diego, California.

Generation 3

6.   **Gilbert Edward Maynard**, son of Edward Maynard and Bertie Payne was born on 19 Apr 1912 in Texas. He died on 06 Apr 1968 in Wylie, Texas. He married **Ina Mae Campbell**, daughter of Arvel Lee Campbell and Hester Maloney Dickerson on 28 Aug 1929 in Rockwall, Texas.

7.   **Ina Mae Campbell**, daughter of Arvel Lee Campbell and Hester Maloney Dickerson was born on 19 Apr 1913 in Greenville, Texas. She died on 19 Oct 2003 in Garland, Texas.

More About Gilbert Edward Maynard:
Burial: 08 Apr 1968 in Wylie Cemetery, Wylie, Texas
Cause Of Death: Myocardiac Infarction
Occupation: Manufacturing Maintenance

More About Ina Mae Campbell:
Burial: Wylie Cemetery, Wylie, Texas

Ina Mae Campbell and Gilbert Edward Maynard had the following child:

i. Billy Edward Maynard, son of Gilbert Edward Maynard and Ina Mae Campbell was born on 14 Jul 1932 in Texas. He married Karen Ann Hensley, daughter of Grover Cecil Hensley and Letha Arwaner White on 24 Dec 1955 in Wylie, Texas. She was born on 17 Jun 1937 in Durant, Oklahoma.

6.   **Grover Cecil Hensley**, son of Floyd Hensley and Exie Beatrice Carter was born on 20 Jul 1911 in Silvey, Oklahoma. He died on 23 Nov 1996 in Alba, Texas. He married **Letha Arwaner White**, daughter of James Lumbus White and Alice Catherine Mack on 15 Aug 1931 in Flosom, Oklahoma.

7.   **Letha Arwaner White**, daughter of James Lumbus White and Alice Catherine Mack was born on 20 Sep 1912 in Kennitick, Oklahoma. She died on 22 Jul 1991 in Leonard, Texas.

More About Grover Cecil Hensley:
Occupation: Machinist
Occupation: Chauffeur

Letha Arwaner White and Grover Cecil Hensley had the following child:

3   i. Karen Ann Hensley, daughter of Grover Cecil Hensley and Letha Arwaner White was born on 17 Jun 1937 in Durant, Oklahoma. She married Billy Edward Maynard, son of Gilbert Edward Maynard and Ina Mae Campbell on 24 Dec 1955 in Wylie, Texas. He was born on 14 Jul 1932 in Texas.

Generation 4

8.   **Edward Maynard**, son of Moses N. Maynard and Mary Wood was born in Dec 1892 in Texas. He died on 27 Dec 1911 in Rockwall, Texas. He married **Bertie Payne** on 13 Jun 1909 in Rockwall, Texas.

9.   **Bertie Payne** was born about 1893 in Texas.

More About Edward Maynard:
Burial: 28 Dec 1911 in Rockwall, Texas

Bertie Payne and Edward Maynard had the following child:

4.   i. Gilbert Edward Maynard, son of Edward Maynard and Bertie Payne was born on 19 Apr 1912 in Texas. He died on 06 Apr 1968 in Wylie, Texas. He married Ina Mae Campbell, daughter of Arvel Lee Campbell and Hester Maloney Dickerson on 28 Aug 1929 in Rockwall, Texas. She was born on 19 Apr 1913 in Greenville, Texas. She died on 19 Oct 2003 in Garland, Texas.

10.   **Arvel Lee Campbell**, son of James W. Campbell and Martha Rush was born on 01 Jul 1886 in Texas. He died on 18 Jun 1955 in Wylie, Texas. He married **Hester Maloney Dickerson**.

11.   **Hester Maloney Dickerson**, daughter of James Dickerson and Lula Provins was born on 09 Jun 1888 in Campbell, Dunkin County, Missouri. She died on 30 May 1975 in Wylie, Texas.

More About Arvel Lee Campbell:
Burial: 19 Jun 1955 in Wylie Cemetery, Wylie, Texas
Occupation: Farmer

More About Hester Maloney Dickerson:
Burial: 01 Jun 1975 in Wylie Cemetery, Wylie, Texas
Cause Of Death: Cerebral Vascular Accident

Hester Maloney Dickerson and Arvel Lee Campbell had the following children:

i.   James Audie Campbell, son of Arvel Lee Campbell and Hester Maloney Dickerson was born on 04 Sep 1908. He died on 20 Oct 1988 in Collin County, Texas. He married Annie Lee webb. She was born on 27 Apr 1908 in Caddo Mills, Hunt County, Texas.

ii.   Ira Edgar Campbell, son of Arvel Lee Campbell and Hester Maloney Dickerson was born on 09 Nov 1910. He died on 02 Dec 1995 in Wylie, Texas. He married Laura Edith Hicks on 04 Sep 1929. She was born on 26 Feb 1910 in Wylie, Texas. She died on 27 Nov 2010.

iii. Ina Mae Campbell, daughter of Arvel Lee Campbell and Hester Maloney Dickerson was born on 19 Apr 1913 in Greenville, Texas. She died on 19 Oct 2003 in Garland, Texas. She married Gilbert Edward Maynard, son of Edward Maynard and Bertie Payne on 28 Aug 1929 in Rockwall, Texas. He was born on 19 Apr 1912 in Texas. He died on 06 Apr 1968 in Wylie, Texas.

Paul Leon Campbell, son of Arvel Lee Campbell and Hester Maloney Dickerson was born on 10 Jun 1915 in Greenville, Texas. He died on 28 Jul 2003 in Garland, Texas. He married Nannie Dell Deen. She was born on 10 Aug 1924. She died on Oct 1997 in Whitesboro, texas. He married Mary Elizabeth Edna Woodard. She was born on 10 Aug 1915. She died on 13 Dec 1986 in Dallas, Texas. He married Martha Elizabeth Stanford. She was born on 01 Oct 1917 in Farmersville, Texas. She died on 09 Jan 2002 in Wylie, Texas.

Edna Elta Campbell, daughter of Arvel Lee Campbell and Hester Maloney Dickerson was born on 28 Mar 1919 in Bryan County, Oklahoma. She married T. J. Henderson.

Jesse C. Campbell, son of Arvel Lee Campbell and Hester Maloney Dickerson was born on 09 Sep 1922 in Texas. He married Martha Irene Luellan. She was born on Jun 1923 in Wylie, Texas.

Earl Vernon Campbell, son of Arvel Lee Campbell and Hester Maloney Dickerson was born on 26 Jan 1925 in Blackwell, Texas. He married Della Jessie McCullough. She was born on 01 Oct 1925 in Tennessee.

12.   **Floyd Hensley**, son of Jim Hensley was born in Kentucky. He married **Exie Beatrice Carter**.

13.   **Exie Beatrice Carter** was born on 11 Feb 1896 in Farmersville, Texas.

More About Floyd Hensley:
Burial: Oak Grove, Oklahoma

More About Exie Beatrice Carter:
Burial: McKinney, Texas

Exie Beatrice Carter and Floyd Hensley had the following child:
6.   i.   Grover Cecil Hensley, son of Floyd Hensley and Exie Beatrice Carter was born on 20 Jul 1911 in Silvey, Oklahoma. He died on 23 Nov 1996 in Alba, Texas. He married Letha Arwaner White, daughter of James Lumbus White and Alice Catherine Mack on 15 Aug 1931 in Flosom, Oklahoma. She was born on 20 Sep 1912 in Kennitick, Oklahoma. She died on 22 Jul 1991 in Leonard, Texas.

14.   **James Lumbus White**, son of William Jackson White and Mary Crosby was born on 14 Jul 1875. He died in Oak Grove, Oklahoma. He married **Alice Catherine Mack**.

15.   **Alice Catherine Mack**, daughter of Moses Mack and Mary Louise Pitts was born on 18 Nov 1872.

Alice Catherine Mack and James Lumbus White had the following child:
7.   i. Letha Arwaner White, daughter of James Lumbus White and Alice Catherine Mack was born on 20 Sep 1912 in Kennitick, Oklahoma. She died on 22 Jul 1991 in Leonard, Texas. She married Grover Cecil Hensley, son of Floyd Hensley and Exie Beatrice Carter on 15 Aug 1931 in Flosom, Oklahoma. He was born on 20 Jul 1911 in Silvey, Oklahoma. He died on 23 Nov 1996 in Alba, Texas.

Generation 5

16.   **Moses N. Maynard**, son of George Lafayette Maynard and Nancy E. Sellers was born about 1868 in Tennessee. He died on 18 Jul 1892 in Wesson, Collin County, Texas. He married **Mary Wood**.

17.   **Mary Wood**.

Mary Wood and Moses N. Maynard had the following children:

8.   i. Edward Maynard, son of Moses N. Maynard and Mary Wood was born in Dec 1892 in Texas. He died on 27 Dec 1911 in Rockwall, Texas. He married Bertie Payne on 13 Jun 1909 in Rockwall, Texas. She was born about 1893 in Texas.

iii. Arthur Lawrence Maynard, son of Moses N. Maynard and Mary Wood was born on Jul 1888 in Texas. He died on 06 Oct 1865 in Wylie, Texas.

More About Arthur Lawrence Maynard:
Burial: 07 Oct 1965 in New Wylie Cemetery, Wylie, Texas
Cause Of Death: Heart Failure
Occupation: Farmer

Notes for Arthur Lawrence Maynard:
World War One draft registration gives birth date as July 1, 1887. Death certificate gives birth date as July 1, 1888. 1900 U.S. census gives birth date as July 1888. Headstone gives birth date as July 1, 1888.

20.   **James W. Campbell** was born in Sep 1851 in Tennessee. He married **Martha Rush**.

21.   **Martha Rush** was born in Mar 1857 in Arkansas.

Martha Rush and James W. Campbell had the following child:

10.   i. Arvel Lee Campbell, son of James W. Campbell and Martha Rush was born on 01 Jul 1886 in Texas. He died on 18 Jun 1955 in Wylie, Texas. He married Hester Maloney Dickerson. She was born on 09 Jun 1888 in Campbell, Dunkin County, Missouri. She died on 30 May 1975 in Wylie, Texas.

22.   **James Dickerson** was born in 1867 in Missouri. He married **Lula Provins**.

23.   **Lula Provins** was born in Missouri.

More About James Dickerson:
Occupation: 1888 in Campbell, Dunkin County, Missouri; Farmer

Lula Provins and James Dickerson had the following child:

11.   i. Hester Maloney Dickerson, daughter of James Dickerson and Lula Provins was born on 09 Jun 1888 in Campbell, Dunkin County, Missouri. She died on 30 May 1975 in Wylie, Texas. She married Arvel Lee Campbell. He was born on 01 Jul 1886 in Texas. He died on 18 Jun 1955 in Wylie, Texas.

24.   **Jim Hensley**.

Jim Hensley had the following child:

12.   i. Floyd Hensley, son of Jim Hensley was born in Kentucky. He married Exie Beatrice Carter. She was born on 11 Feb 1896 in Farmersville, Texas.

28   **William Jackson White** was born on 03 Jul 1846. He died in 1919 in Oak Grove, Oklahoma. He married **Mary Crosby**.

29   **Mary Crosby** was born in 1844 in Arkansas. She died in 1916.

Mary Crosby and William Jackson White had the following child:

14.   i.   James Lumbus White, son of William Jackson White and Mary Crosby was born on 14 Jul 1875. He died in Oak Grove, Oklahoma. He married Alice Catherine Mack. She was born on 18 Nov 1872.

30. **Moses Mack**. He died on 21 Oct 1889. He married **Mary Louise Pitts**.

31. **Mary Louise Pitts**. She died on 22 Apr 1896.

Mary Louise Pitts and Moses Mack had the following child:

15.   i.   Alice Catherine Mack, daughter of Moses Mack and Mary Louise Pitts was born on 18 Nov 1872. She married James Lumbus White. He was born on 14 Jul 1875. He died in Oak Grove, Oklahoma.

Generation 6

32. **George Lafayette Maynard**, son of Shadrach Maynard and Elizabeth French was born on 03 Dec 1846 in Jefferson County, Tennessee. He died on 10 Jan 1907 in Bowie, Texas. He married **Nancy E. Sellers**, daughter of Samuel Sellers and Emily A. (unknown) on 03 Mar 1867 in Jefferson County, Tennessee.

33. **Nancy E. Sellers**, daughter of Samuel Sellers and Emily A. (unknown) was born about 1846 in Tennessee. She died about 1880.

More About George Lafayette Maynard:
Burial: 11 Jan 1907 in Elmwood Cemetery, Bowie, Texas
Cause Of Death: Tuberculosis
Occupation: Sawmill Worker in 1880

Nancy E. Sellers and George Lafayette Maynard had the following children:

16.   i.   Moses N. Maynard, son of George Lafayette Maynard and Nancy E. Sellers was born about 1868 in Tennessee. He died on 18 Jul 1892 in Wesson, Collin County, Texas. He married Mary Wood.

      ii.   Texanna Belle Maynard, daughter of George Lafayette Maynard and Nancy E. Sellers was born on 30 Nov 1869 in Tennessee. She died on 15 May 1957 in Bowie, Texas. She married Elijah Richard Wauford.

          More About Texanna Belle Maynard: Burial:
Elmwood Cemetery, Bowie, Texas

      iii.   Shadrach S. Maynard, son of George Lafayette Maynard and Nancy E. Sellers was born on 06 Dec 1871 in Jefferson County, Tennessee. He died on 15 Dec 1939 in Rockwall, Texas. He married Katy Lowry on 04 May 1891 in Rockwall, Texas.

          More About Shadrach S. Maynard:
Burial: Rockwall City Cemetery, Rockwall, Texas

      iv.   Caroline Maynard, daughter of George Lafayette Maynard and Nancy E. Sellers was born about 1874 in Tennessee. She died in 1945.

      v.   Nellie Maynard, daughter of George Lafayette Maynard and Nancy E. Sellers was born on 12 May 1877 in Jefferson County, Tennessee. She died on 15 Aug 1967 in Oklahoma City, Oklahoma.

      vi.   Mary Emma Maynard, daughter of George Lafayette Maynard and Nancy E. Sellers was born in Feb 1880 in Tennessee.

Generation 7

64.   **Shadrach Maynard**, son of Gibson Maynard and Delilah Cate was born on 18 Nov 1810 in Dandridge, Tennessee. He died on 03 Sep 1882 in Tennessee. He married **Elizabeth French**, daughter of Moses French and Sarah E. Elder in 1835 in Tennessee.

65.   **Elizabeth French**, daughter of Moses French and Sarah E. Elder was born in 1816 in Tennessee. She died in 1865 in Jefferson City, Tennessee.

Elizabeth French and Shadrach Maynard had the following children:

      i.   Sarah Maynard, daughter of Shadrach Maynard and Elizabeth French was born in 1835.

      ii.   Phebe Maynard, daughter of Shadrach Maynard and Elizabeth French was born in 1840.

      iii.   James C. Maynard, son of Shadrach Maynard and Elizabeth French was born in 1843.

      iv.   Celah Maynard, child of Shadrach Maynard and Elizabeth French was born in 1845.

33.   v. George Lafayette Maynard, son of Shadrach Maynard and Elizabeth French was born on 03 Dec 1846 in Jefferson County, Tennessee. He died on 10 Jan 1907 in Bowie, Texas. He married Nancy E. Sellers, daughter of Samuel Sellers and Emily A. (unknown) on 03 Mar 1867 in Jefferson County, Tennessee. She was born about 1846 in Tennessee. She died about 1880. He married Sally Parker on 16 Jul 1883 in Collin County, Texas.

      vi.   William Maynard, son of Shadrach Maynard and Elizabeth French was born in 1849.

      vii.   Shadrack M. Maynard, son of Shadrach Maynard and Elizabeth French was born in 1851. He died in 1922.

      viii.   E. Maynard, son of Shadrach Maynard and Elizabeth French was born in 1853.

66.   **Samuel Sellers**. He married **Emily A. (unknown)**.

67.   **Emily A. (unknown)**.

Emily A. (unknown) and Samuel Sellers had the following child:

33.   i. Nancy E. Sellers, daughter of Samuel Sellers and Emily A. (unknown) was born about 1846 in Tennessee. She died about 1880. She married George Lafayette Maynard, son of Shadrach Maynard and Elizabeth French on 03 Mar 1867 in Jefferson County, Tennessee. He was born on 03 Dec 1846 in Jefferson County, Tennessee. He died on 10 Jan 1907 in Bowie, Texas.

Generation 8

128   **Gibson Maynard** was born in 1778 in Wilkes County, North Carolina. He died on 12 Dec 1842 in Adams County, Illinois. He married **Delilah Cate**, daughter of Charles Cate and Sarah Baldwin in 1799 in Jefferson County, Tennessee.

129   **Delilah Cate**, daughter of Charles Cate and Sarah Baldwin was born in 1781 in Wilkes County, North Carolina. She died in 1870 in Adams County, Illinois.

Delilah Cate and Gibson Maynard had the following children:

    i.   Levi Maynard, son of Gibson Maynard and Delilah Cate was born in 1800. He died in 1850.

    ii.   Daniel Maynard, son of Gibson Maynard and Delilah Cate was born in 1803.

    iii.   Rebecca Maynard, daughter of Gibson Maynard and Delilah Cate was born in 1805.

64.   iv. Shadrach Maynard, son of Gibson Maynard and Delilah Cate was born on 18 Nov 1810 in Dandridge, Tennessee. He died on 03 Sep 1882 in Tennessee. He married Elizabeth French, daughter of Moses French and Sarah E. Elder in 1835 in Tennessee. She was born in 1816 in Tennessee. She died in 1865 in Jefferson City, Tennessee. He married Nancy H. (unknown). She was born about 1827 in Tennessee.

    v.   Meshack Maynard, son of Gibson Maynard and Delilah Cate was born in 1813.

    vi.   Abednego Maynard, son of Gibson Maynard and Delilah Cate was born in 1815. He died in 1872.

    vii.   Phebe Jane Maynard, daughter of Gibson Maynard and Delilah Cate was born in 1817.

    viii.   Cella Maynard, daughter of Gibson Maynard and Delilah Cate was born in 1824.

    ix.   Lydia Maynard, daughter of Gibson Maynard and Delilah Cate was born in 1825.

    x.   William Maynard, son of Gibson Maynard and Delilah Cate was born in 1827. He died in 1880.

    xi.   Darcus Maynard, son of Gibson Maynard and Delilah Cate was born in 1829. He died in 1900.

130.   **Moses French** was born on 14 Aug 1791 in Spartanburg, South Carolina. He died in 1874 in Jefferson County, Tennessee. He married **Sarah E. Elder**.

131.   **Sarah E. Elder** was born in 1794 in North Carolina. She died in Sep 1847 in Jefferson County, Tennessee.

Sarah E. Elder and Moses French had the following child:

65.   i. Elizabeth French, daughter of Moses French and Sarah E. Elder was born in 1816 in Tennessee. She died in 1865 in Jefferson City, Tennessee. She married Shadrach Maynard, son of Gibson Maynard and Delilah Cate in 1835 in Tennessee. He was born on 18 Nov 1810 in Dandridge, Tennessee. He died on 03 Sep 1882 in Tennessee.

Generation 9

258.   **Charles Cate** was born in 1739 in Bertie, North Carolina. He died on 12 Jan 1811 in Jefferson County, Tennessee. He married **Sarah Baldwin**.

259.   **Sarah Baldwin** was born in 1745. She died in 1796.

Sarah Baldwin and Charles Cate had the following child:

129.   i. Delilah Cate, daughter of Charles Cate and Sarah Baldwin was born in 1781 in Wilkes County, North Carolina. She died in 1870 in Adams County, Illinois. She

---

married Gibson Maynard in 1799 in Jefferson County, Tennessee. He was born in 1778 in Wilkes County, North Carolina. He died on 12 Dec 1842 in Adams County, Illinois.

Descendants of Billy Darrell Maynard

Generation 1

1. **BILLY DARRELL**[1] **MAYNARD** was born on 05 Nov 1956 in McKinney, Texas. He married Barbara Ann Bell, daughter of William Robert Bell and Alma Louise Akerman on 14 Oct 1976 in Wylie, Texas. She was born on 07 Jun 1958 in San Diego, California.

More About Billy Darrell Maynard:
Occupation: Machinist

Billy Darrell Maynard and Barbara Ann Bell had the following children:

> i. **BRYAN JUSTIN**[2] **MAYNARD** was born on 09 Apr 1983 in Quitman, Texas. He married Sarah Marie Hickey, daughter of Dan Patrick Hickey and Tracey Ann Blakely on 05 Aug 2005 in Havelock, North Carolina. She was born on 17 Mar 1984 in Kansas City, Missouri.

> ii. **BRANDON MAYNARD** was born on 01 Jan 1988 in Garland, Texas. He married Jessica Raye Penney, daughter of Dean Penney and Billye Turnbow Stark on 10 Nov 2012 in Farmersville, Texas. She was born on 18 Oct 1987.

Generation 2

2. **BRYAN JUSTIN**[2] **MAYNARD** (Billy Darrell[1]) was born on 09 Apr 1983 in Quitman, Texas. He married Sarah Marie Hickey, daughter of Dan Patrick Hickey and Tracey Ann Blakely on 05 Aug 2005 in Havelock, North Carolina. She was born on 17 Mar 1984 in Kansas City, Missouri.

More About Bryan Justin Maynard:
Military Service: U. S. Marines

Bryan Justin Maynard and Sarah Marie Hickey had the following children:

> i. **WILLIAM PATRICK**[3] **MAYNARD** was born on 27 Aug 2007 in New Bern, North Carolina.

> ii. **EMMA JUNE MAYNARD** was born on 04 Jul 2008 in Portsmouth, Virginia. She died on 04 Jul 2008 in Portsmouth, Virginia.

3. **BRANDON**[2] **MAYNARD** (Billy Darrell[1]) was born on 01 Jan 1988 in Garland, Texas. He married Jessica Raye Penney, daughter of Dean Penney and Billye Turnbow Stark on 10 Nov 2012 in Farmersville, Texas. She was born on 18 Oct 1987.

Brandon Maynard and Jessica Raye Penney had the following child:

> i. **CONNER**[3] **MAYNARD** was born on 22 Jul 2014 in Allen, Collin County, Texas.

Sarah, Bryan and William Maynard

Brandon and Jessica Maynard

NOTES:

NOTES: